Franklin Fiske Heard

Shakespeare as a Lawyer

Franklin Fiske Heard

Shakespeare as a Lawyer

ISBN/EAN: 9783337791315

Printed in Europe, USA, Canada, Australia, Japan

Cover: Foto ©Thomas Meinert / pixelio.de

More available books at **www.hansebooks.com**

SHAKESPEARE

AS A

LAWYER

BY

FRANKLIN FISKE HEARD

BOSTON

LITTLE, BROWN, AND COMPANY

1883

Cambridge:

PRINTED BY JOHN WILSON AND SON,

UNIVERSITY PRESS.

I am a wise fellow, and one that knows the law.

MUCH ADO ABOUT NOTHING. Act iv. sc. 2.

I was once at Clements-inn.

Second Part of KING HENRY IV. Act iii. sc. 2.

Faith, I have been a truant in the law,
And never yet could frame my will to it.

First Part of KING HENRY VI. Act ii. sc. 4.

But in these nice sharp quillets of the law,
Good faith, I am no wiser than a daw.

First Part of KING HENRY VI. Act ii. sc. 4.

Thou art clerkly, thou art clerkly.

THE MERRY WIVES OF WINDSOR. Act iv. sc. 5.

PREFACE.

I AM aware that the attempt made in this volume has been anticipated by others. The notes of critics and commentators upon Shakespeare, superfluously full in certain particulars, are singularly meagre in pointing out and explaining his references to the technical science of the Law. And yet the room for such reference is abundant.

In selecting the passages and the illustrations and criticisms thereon, which will be found in the following pages, constant use has been made of the various editions of Shakespeare. I have not relied upon my own complete perusal of his Works. From

the wealth of material I have made a copious selection. In the language of Lambard,

" If I shall be thoughte to have heaped up
too many conceites, I make answere that I
have omitted manye, and have made the best
choice that I could. Moreover, I will no lesse
gladly be admonished of my mistakings, than
readily reforme them."

In printing the quotations I have, in general, followed the text of the Third Edition
of Dyce.

BOSTON, October, 1883.

SHAKESPEARE AS A LAWYER.

CHAPTER I.

"ALL that is known with any degree of certainty concerning Shakespeare, is, that he was born at Stratford-upon-Avon; married and had children there; went to London, where he commenced actor, and wrote poems and plays; returned to Stratford, made his will, died, and was buried." The Rev. Alexander Dyce says, "Such is the remark made long ago by one of the most acute of his commentators; and even at the present day, — notwithstanding some additional notices of Shakespeare which have

Steevens.

Dyce.

been more recently discovered, — the truth of the remark can hardly fail to be felt and acknowledged by all, except by professed antiquaries, with whom the mere mention of a name, in whatever kind of document, assumes the character of an important fact."

In 1790 Malone — himself a barrister, whose services, whether as biographer or commentator, have never been adequately acknowledged — published his first edition of Shakespeare's Works. It was his opinion, an opinion subsequently adopted by several other critics, that some years of Shakespeare's youth were passed in an attorney's office. He observes that the Poet's "knowledge of legal terms is not merely such as might be acquired by the casual observation of even his all-comprehending mind; it has the appearance of *technical* skill; and he is so fond of displaying it on all occasions, that I suspect he was early initiated in at least the forms of law, and was employed, while he yet remained at Stratford, in the office of some country attorney, who was

Malone.

Collier.

Legal Terms.

at the same time a petty conveyancer, and perhaps also the seneschal of some manor court." There can be no doubt that legal expressions are more frequent, and are used with more precision, in his writings than in those of any other dramatic author of the period. " The technical language of the law runs from his pen as part of his vocabulary and parcel of his thought." A professional acquaintance with the law is certainly indicated by his familiarity with the technical terms and phrases of its most intricate branches, — the law of real property and the law of pleading, — terms and phrases which he uses " with an air of as entire unconsciousness as if they were a part of the language of his daily life."

Lord Campbell, the Lord Chief Justice of the Queen's Bench, in summing up the evidence in the case, said: " I am amazed not only at the number of Shakespeare's juridical phrases and forensic allusions, but by the accuracy and propriety with which they are uniformly introduced. While novelists and

*Collier.
Staunton.*

R. G. White.

Lord Campbell.

dramatists are constantly making mistakes as to the law of marriage, of wills, and of inheritance, to Shakespeare's law, lavishly as he propounds it, there can neither be demurrer, nor bill of exceptions, nor writ of error." There is a seemingly utter impossibility of his having acquired, on any other theory, than that of having studied the law, "the marvellous intimacy which he displays with legal terms, his frequent adoption of them in illustration, and his curiously technical knowledge of their form and force," which no mere quickness of intuition can account for. "Genius, though it reveals general and even particular truths, and facilitates all acquirement, does not impart facts or the knowledge of technical terms." If these inquiries do not prove that "in hot blood he stepp'd into the law," they help to show with what masterly comprehensiveness he could deal with the peculiarities of this, as of nearly every other human pursuit. Indeed, he confesses, —

> I have been a truant in the law,
> And never yet could frame my will to it.

Charles and
Mary Cowden
Clarke.

White.

Staunton.

Authors do not use technical terms in the familiar way in which Shakespeare speaks of the law, unless the terms really are familiar to them by frequent use; and we find these terms and allusions used by him in an apparently unconscious way, as the natural turn of his thoughts. Among these, there are some which few but a lawyer would, and some even which none but a lawyer could, have written. Of course they are necessarily short and incomplete, for it is not in a tragedy or comedy that we should expect to find a technical description of the law or any other profession.

This question can be decided by the internal evidence afforded by the Poet's writings. When Malone published his theory, he cited in support of it twenty-four passages. Subsequent writers have cited a much larger number, many of which are impertinent and immaterial.

Cf. "Shakespeare as an Angler," by Rev. H. N. Ellacombe, pp. 9, 10, 24.

CHAPTER II.

IN " The Merry Wives of Windsor," Act II. sc. 2, where Ford, disguised, tries to induce Falstaff to assist him in his intrigue with Mrs. Ford, and states that for all the money and trouble he had bestowed upon her he had received no satisfaction, nor promise of any at her hands, there is this passage : —

FAL. Of what quality was your love, then ?
FORD. Like a fair house, built on another man's ground ; *so that I have lost my edifice by mistaking the place where I erected it.*

First Parish in Sudbury *v.* Jones, 8 Cush. 184, 189.

In 1852 by a decision of the Supreme Judicial Court of Massachusetts, the town of Sudbury in the county of Middlesex, lost a school-house " by mistaking the place where they erected it." The term " land " legally includes all houses and buildings standing thereon. Whatever is affixed to the realty is thereby made parcel thereof, and belongs to the owner of the soil. Quicquid plantatur solo, solo cedit. Buildings erected on land of another voluntarily and without any contract with the owner become 'part. of the real estate, and belong to the owner of the soil. Although the principle is one of great antiquity, yet it is so far technical, that it is not familiar to unprofessional persons.

Co. Litt. 4 a.
Wentw. Off. Ex.
14th ed. 145.
Angus *v.* Dalton, 6 App.
Cas. 740.

In Riddle *v.* Welden, it was decided that the goods of a boarder are not liable to be distrained for rent due by the keeper of the boarding-house. Chief Justice Gibson, in delivering the opinion of the court, said that Falstaff "speaks with legal precision when he demands, 'Shall I not take mine ease in mine inn.'" In early times an *inn* signified a dwelling; and "To take mine ease in mine inne" was an ancient proverb, says Percy, not

5 Wharton, 15.

Henry IV.
Part I., Act
III. sc. 3.

Inne.

very different, in its application, from that
maxim, " Every man's house is his castle; "
for *inne* originally signified *a house* or *habi-
tation* [Sax., inne, domus, domicilium]. When
the word *inne* began to change its meaning,
and to be used to signify *a house of entertainment*, the proverb, still continuing in force,
was applied in the latter sense, as it is here
used by Shakespeare.

An example of the use of the word, in its
early signification, occurs in Greene's " Fare-
well to Folly" (1591): " The beggar Irus,
that haunted the palace of Penelope, would
take his ease in his inne, as well as the peers
of Ithaca."

The Reporters,
275, 4th ed.

When Mr. Justice Shallow, grieved by the
" disparagements of Falstaff," threatened to
" make a Star-Chamber matter of it," vowing
that " if he were twenty Sir John Falstaffs, he
should not abuse Robert Shallow, Esquire,"
— who writes himself " Armigero," — he
seems to have apprehended, with judicial ex-

actness, the extraordinary jurisdiction of this
tribunal; slanderous words against a king's
justice being one of the offences specially
punished by the Star Chamber, in exercise of
a peculiar as distinguished from an ordinary
jurisdiction. And the charity of Sir Hugh,
the parson, was much better than his law,
when he supposed that the council desired
"to hear the fear of Got, and not to hear a
riot;" unlawful assemblies, routs, *riots*, for-
geries, perjuries, cozoanges, and libellings,
being declared in the Reports known as
"Star-Chamber Cases," to be the matters
which properly belong to the jurisdiction of
the Star Chamber.

Star Chamber.

An exception to the rule rejecting hearsay
evidence is allowed in the case of *dying decla-
rations.* Shakespeare, in "King John," has
put the principle on which this species of
evidence is admitted into the mouth of the
wounded Melun, who, finding himself disbe-

*Dying declara-
tions.
Best Ev. § 505.*

lieved while announcing the intended treach-
ery of the Dauphin Lewis, exclaims : —

Have I not hideous death within my view,
Retaining but a quantity of life,
Which bleeds away, even as a form of wax
Resolveth from his figure 'gainst the fire?
What in the world should make me now deceive,
Since I must lose the use of all deceit?
Why should I, then, be false, since it is true
That I must die here, and live hence by truth?

Act v. sc. 4.

The King *v.*
Woodcock, 1
Leach C.C. 502.

Evidence of this description is admissible
only in the single instance of homicide,
" where the death of the deceased is the subject of the charge, and the circumstances of
the death are the subject of the dying decla-
ration."   One reason for thus restricting the
admission of this species of evidence may be
the experienced fact, that implicit reliance
cannot in all cases be placed on the declara-
tions of a dying person; for his body may
have survived the powers of his mind. Thus,
in " King John," Prince Henry says : —

The King *v.*
Mead, 2 B. & C.
608, and 4 D. &
R. 120. Regina
v. Hind, Bell
C. C. 253.

O vanity of sickness ! fierce extremes
In their continuance will not feel themselves.
Death, having prey'd upon the outward parts,
Leaves them insensible ; and 's siege is now
Against the mind, the which he pricks and wounds
With many legions of strange fantasies,
Which, in their throng and press to that last hold,
Confound themselves.   Act v. sc. 7.

In " King Henry VIII." there is an accurate statement of the nature of a writ of præmunire, and of the punishment consequent upon conviction thereon. " Præmunire is a writ, and it lieth where any man sueth any other in the Spiritual Court for any thing that is determinable in the King's Court." The punishment of this offence, as prescribed by the different statutes, is thus shortly summed up by Lord Coke: " That, from the conviction, the defendant *shall be out of the king's protection, and his lands and tenements, goods and chattels, forfeited to the king.*" The writ was intended to prevent the abuse of spiritual power. The Duke

Præmunire.

Termes de la Ley.

1 Inst. 129 b.

of Suffolk, addressing Cardinal Wolsey, says, —

> Lord cardinal, the king's further pleasure is, —
> Because all those things you have done of late,
> By your *power legatine, within this kingdom,*
> Fall into the compass of a *præmunire,* —
> That therefore such a writ be su'd against you ;
> *To forfeit all your goods, lands, tenements,*
> *Chattels, and whatsoever, and to be*
> *Out of the king's protection :* — this is my charge.
>
> Act iii. sc. 2.

Although the purpose of the writ of præmunire, and the punishment incident to conviction, are thus technically stated, still it is by no means certain, that Shakespeare acquired this knowledge in the course of his professional reading. From the following passages in Holinshed, it will be seen that Shakespeare merely versified that author : —

Holinshed.

In the meane time the king, being informed that all those things that the cardinall had doone by his *power legantine within this realme, were in the case of the premunire and prouision,* caused his atturneie Christopher Hales *to sue out a writ of premunire against him.* — Vol. iii. p. 740, ed. 1807–8.

After this, in the king's bench his matter for the premunire, being called vpon, two atturneis, which he had authorised by his warrant signed with his owne hand, confessed the action, and so had iudgement *to forfeit all his lands, tenements, goods, and cattels, and to be out of the king's protection. — Ib.* p. 741.

To "sue out livery" is to institute a suit by a ward of the crown, on arriving at legal age, to obtain possession of his lands, which the king had held as guardian in chivalry. As this was not done until a minor came of age, the phrase was occasionally used as an expression to denote majority. Thus, Donne, who had been a student at Lincoln's Inn, and afterwards elected preacher to the Society, wrote : —

> Our little Cupid hath *sued livery*,
> And is no more in his minority.
> *Eclogue,* 1613.

And Fletcher, in " The Woman's Prize : " —

> If Cupid
> Shoots arrows of that weight, I 'll swear devoutly
> H 'as *sued his livery*, and is no more a boy.
> Act ii. sc. 1.

Sidenotes: Sue out livery. Donne. Fletcher.

To "sue out livery" was a writ of *ouster le main*, that is, his *livery*, that the king's hand might be taken off, and the land *delivered* to him.   York says to Richard II., —

> If you do wrongfully seize Hereford's rights,
> Call in the letters-patents that he hath
> By his *attorneys-general to sue*
> *His livery*, and deny his offer'd homage,
> You pluck a thousand dangers on your head.
> *Richard II.* Act ii. sc. 1.

And in the third scene of the same act, Bolingbroke says, —

> I am denied *to sue my livery* here,
> And yet my letters-patents give me leave:
> My father's *goods are all distrain'd* and sold;
> And these and all are all amiss employ'd.
> What would you have me do?   I am a subject,
> And challenge law: *attorneys are* denied me;
> And therefore *personally* I lay my claim
> To my inheritance of free descent.

Hotspur, in giving a description of Henry the Fourth's condition, when he landed at Ravenspurg, refers to the same act of Richard II. toward Bolingbroke: —

> He came but to be Duke of Lancaster,
> To *sue his livery* and beg his peace.
> *First Part of Henry IV.* Act iv. sc. 3.

The corresponding passage in Holinshed, which Shakespeare dramatized in " Richard II.," is as follows : —

In this meane time, the duke of Lancaster departed out of this life at the bishop of Elies place in Holborne, and lieth buried in the cathedrall church of saint Paule in London, on the northside of the high altar, by the ladie Blanch his first wife. The death of this duke gaue occasion of increasing more hatred in the people of this realme toward the king, for he seized into his hands all the goods that belonged to him, and also receiued all the rents and reuenues of his lands which ought to haue descended vnto the duke of Hereford by lawfull *inheritance*, in reuoking his *letters patents*, which he had granted to him before, by vertue wherof he might make his attorneis generall *to sue liuerie* for him, of any maner of *inheritances* or possessions that might from thenceforth fall vnto him, and that his *homage* might be respited, with making reasonable fine : whereby it was euident, that the king meant his vtter vndooing. — Vol. ii. p. 849, ed. 1807–8.

" Livery of seisin " is a delivery of possession of lands, tenements, and hereditaments, to one who has a right to the same. It is a ceremony of the common law, used in the conveyance of lands. *Livery* and *seisin* are delivery and possession. In Webster's "The Devil's Law Case," Act i. sc. 2, Romelio says, —

> Keep your possession, you leave the door by the ring;
> That 's *livery and seisin* in England.

At common law, on conveyance of lands, houses, &c., the ring or latch of the door is delivered to the feoffee. Spenser uses this legal term : —

> Therefore inclyning to his goodly reason,
> Agreeing well both with the place and season,
> She gladly did of that same babe accept,
> As of her owne by *liverey and seisin.*

In the Court of Queen's Bench, according to Lord Campbell, when a complaint is made against a person for a "contempt," the practice is, that, before sentence is finally pronounced, he is sent into the crown office, and being there "*charged upon interrogatories*," he is made to swear that he will "*answer all things faithfully*." Accordingly, in the moon-

"The Devil's Law Case."

Faërie Queene. Bk. vi. c. iv. st. 37.

A "contempt."

Charged upon interrogatories.

light scene in the garden at Belmont, after a partial explanation between Bassanio, Gratiano, Portia, and Nerissa, about their rings, some further inquiry being deemed necessary, Portia says, —

> Let us go in ;
> And *charge us there upon inter'gatories*,
> And *we will answer all things faithfully.*

, Gratiano assents, observing, —

> Let it be so : *the first inter'gatory*
> That my Nerissa *shall be sworn on is,*
> Whether till the next night she had rather stay,
> Or go to bed now, being two hours to day.
> > *The Merchant of Venice*, Act v. sc. 1.

To "lay by the heels" was the technical expression for committing to prison. The case of the Mayor of Hereford is thus reported in Salkeld: "Per HOLT C. J. The Mayor of Hereford was *laid by the heels*, for sitting in judgment in a cause where he himself was lessor of the plaintiff in ejectment, though he by charter was sole judge of the

" To lay by the heels."

1 Salk. 396.

court." In " Henry VIII." the lord chamber-
lain says, —

> As I live,
> If the king blame me for 't, I 'll *lay ye all
> By the heels*, and suddenly ; and on your heads
> Clap round fines for neglect.　　　*Act v. sc. 3.*

And the Chief Justice to Falstaff : —

> To punish you *by the heels* would amend the
> attention of your ears ; and I care not if I do be-
> come your physician. — *Second Part of Henry IV.*
> Act i. sc. 2.

Nares's Glossa-
ry, *s.v.*
" Charge."

To *charge* his fellows seems to have been
a regular part of the duty of the constable of
the watch. In " Much Ado About Nothing,"
Dogberry, in his " charge " to the watchmen,
uses the precise words of the oath adminis-
tered to the grand jury in England and in
this country at the present day : —

> Keep your fellows' counsels and your own.
> 　　　　　　　　　　　　　　*Act iii. sc. 3.*

Curious as the charge is, it appears to satisfy
the watchmen, whose resolution is as useful
as that is sagacious : —

Well, masters, we hear our *charge :* let us go sit here upon the church-bench till two, and then all to bed. — Act iii. sc. 3.

The word *purchase*, in its common and confined acceptation, is now applied only to such acquisitions of land as are obtained by way of bargain and sale for money, or other valuable consideration. But much oftener in our old writers simply to acquire, being properly to hunt; and then to take in hunting; and then, as the commonest way of acquiring is by giving money in exchange, to buy. Thus, Lord Bacon: "And therefore true consideration of estate can hardly find what to reject, in matter of territory, in any empire, except it be some glorious acquests obtained sometime in the bravery of wars, which cannot be kept without excessive charge and trouble; of which kind were the *purchases* of King Henry VIII. that of Tournay and that of Bologne." In its legal acceptation, "to purchase" is to acquire real estate by means other than by descent or

Purchase.

" Of the True Greatness of the Kingdom of Britain." Works, vol. vii. p. 54, ed. Spedding.

inheritance. If one *gives* land freely to another, he is, in the eye of the law, a purchaser. A man who has his father's estate
settled upon him in tail, before he was born,
is also a purchaser; for he takes quite another estate than the law of descents would
have given him. And even if the ancestor
devises his estate to his heir-at-law by will,
with other limitations, *or* in any other shape,
than the course of descents would direct,
such heir takes by purchase. In "Antony
and Cleopatra" the word is used in its legal
sense. Lepidus, in palliating the faults of
"A man who is the abstract of all faults,"
says, —

> His faults, in him, seem as the spots of heaven,
> More fiery by night's blackness ; *hereditary*,
> Rather than *purchas'd*.   Act. i. sc. 4.

Injuria illata judici seu locum tenenti
regis videtur ipsi regi illata, maxime si
fiat, in exercente officium, is a maxim of
the law.

Shakespeare, in the following passage from " The Second Part of Henry IV.," refers to this maxim, or to the law which it describes : —

> CHIEF JUSTICE. I then did use the person of your father ;
> The image of his power lay then in me :
> And in th' administration of his law,
> Whiles I was busy for the commonwealth,
> Your highness pleasèd to forget my place,
> The majesty and power of law and justice,
> The image of the king whom I presented,
> And struck me in my very seat of judgment ;
> Whereon, as an offender to your father,
> I gave bold way to my authority,
> And did commit you.   Act v. sc. 2.

In a recent case in the House of Lords, Lord Selborne, in the course of the argument as to notice, referred to the case of Chief Justice Gascoigne, who without a moment's hesitation, and without any prior notification, sent the Prince of Wales instantly to the Fleet Prison for a contempt of court committed in præsentiâ; the heir of the crown submitting patiently to the sentence, and making reparation for his error by acknowledging it.

Walt *v.* Ligertwood, L. R. 2 H. L. Sc. App. 367 note.

Cheaters was the popular name for *escheaters*, those officers employed to certify to the Chancery or Exchequer what *escheats* fall to the crown through forfeiture, the death of tenants without heirs, &c. An escheater was an official who appears to have been regarded by the common people, in Shakespeare's day, much the same as they now look upon an informer. In "The Merry Wives of Windsor," Act i. sc. 3, Falstaff, speaking of "Ford's wife" and "Page's wife," says, "I will be *cheater* to them both, and they shall be *exchequers* to me." And in Sonnet CLI. is this line, —

> Then, gentle *cheater*, urge not my amiss,

in which "cheater" signifies *escheater*.

In delineating the character of "that dear simpleton," Sir Andrew Ague-cheek, Shakespeare causes him to suppose that *son assault demesne* is not a good plea to an action of trespass for an assault and battery. After fighting with Sebastian, Sir Andrew says, —

I 'll have an action of battery against him, if there be any law in Illyria: *though I struck him first, yet it's no matter for that.* — *Twelfth Night,* Act iv. sc. 1.

If, at the trial of a case, a question of law arises, the course is for the judge to decide it. But it may happen that one of the parties is dissatisfied with the decision, and may wish to have it revised by a court of superior jurisdiction. For this purpose, it becomes necessary to put the question of law on record for the information of that court. The party excepting to the opinion of the judge tenders him *a bill of exceptions;* that is, a statement in writing of the objection made by the party to his decision ; to which statement, if truly made, the judge is bound to set his seal, in confirmation of its accuracy.

In " Twelfth Night" Maria says to Sir Toby:

By my troth, Sir Toby, you must come in earlier o' nights : your cousin, my lady, *takes great exceptions* to your ill hours.

SIR TOBY.   Why, let her *except before excepted.*

Act i. sc. 3.

Generes *v.* Campbell, 11 Wallace, 193.

Bill of Exceptions.

"This is a whimsical use of a law-phrase,"
says Mr. Grant White, "which is one of the
numberless evidences of Shakespeare's familiarity with the forms of that profession."

The picture in "Coriolanus" which Shake-
speàre drew of the two tribunes, Sicinius and
Brutus, is not without application to certain
judges of the present day. Menenius thus
reproaches the tribunes:—

> You wear out a good wholesome forenoon in
> hearing a cause between an orange-wife and a
> fosset-seller; and then rejourn the controversy of
> three-pence to a second day of audience. When
> you are hearing a matter between party and party,
> if you chance to be pinched with the colic, you
> make faces like mummers; set up the bloody flag
> against all patience; and, in roaring for a chamber-
> pot, dismiss the controversy bleeding, the more en-
> tangled by your hearing: all the peace you make in
> their cause is, calling both the parties knaves.
>
> Act ii. sc. i.

Justices of the peace.

Shakespeare says that justices of the peace
attested the most absurd stories with their

signatures.   Thus, in "The Winter's Tale," Act iv. sc. 3 : —

AUT.   Here's another ballad, Of a fish, that appeared upon the coast on Wednesday the fourscore of April, forty thousand fathom above water, and sung this ballad against the hard hearts of maids : it was thought that she was a woman, and was turned into a cold fish for she would not exchange flesh with one that loved her : the ballad is very pitiful, and as true.

DOR.   Is it true too, think you ?

AUT.   *Five justices' hands at it;* and witnesses more than my pack will hold.

Lord Coke, in the "Fourth Institute," commenting on the jurisdiction and power of justices of the peace, says : " It is such a form of subordinate government for the tranquillity and quiet of the realm, as no part of the Christian world hath the like, if the same be duly executed." Shakespeare's picture of a justice of the peace, in the opening scene of " The Merry Wives of Windsor," certainly differs from the office so unduly commended, in language so extravagantly flattering, by

4 Inst. 170.

the Lord Chief Justice. It has been well said that Shakespeare's picture "is so truthful as to be hardly exaggerated or caricatured. The original of that picture is confined to no age."

In the reign of Elizabeth, actions for slanderous words were of frequent occurrence; and many refined distinctions were resorted to by the judges. To call a man a cuckold was not an ecclesiastical slander: but wittol was; for it imports his knowledge of and consent to his wife's adultery. Shakespeare noticed this distinction. In "The Merry Wives of Windsor," Act ii. sc. 2, Ford exclaims, —

Holt C. J. in Smith *v.* Wood, 2 Salk. 692.

Terms ! names ! — Amaimon sounds well ; Lucifer, well ; Barbason, well ; yet they are devils' additions, the names of fiends : but cuckold ! *wittol-* cuckold ! the devil himself hath not such a name.

"Character 32" (1631), quoted in Nares's Glossary, 2d ed.

"A cuckold," says Lenton, "is a harmelesse horned creature; but they [his horns] hang not in his eies, as your *wittals* doe."

Formerly, when sentence of death was pronounced, the criminal was said to be *attainted*, attinctus, stained, or blackened. "This is after *judgment;* for there is great difference," says Blackstone, "between a man *convicted* and *attainted*, though they are frequently through inaccuracy confounded together." The consequences of attainder were forfeiture and corruption of blood. In "The First Part of King Henry VI.," Act ii. sc. 4, Richard Plantagenet is asked, —

Attainder.

4 Bl. Comm. 381.

> Was not thy father, Richard Earl of Cambridge,
> For treason executed in our late king's days?
> And, by his treason, stand'st thou not *attainted*,
> Corrupted, and exempt from ancient gentry?
> His trespass yet lives guilty in thy blood;
> And, till thou be restor'd, thou art a yeoman.
> PLAN. My father was *attachèd*, not *attainted;*
> Condemn'd to die for treason, but no traitor.

Attainder, forfeiture, and corruption of blood have been entirely abolished.

In "The Winter's Tale," Act i. sc. 2, there is an allusion to that abuse in English law procedure which first lighted the flame of philanthropy in the bosom of Howard, — the dragging back acquitted prisoners to their cells, in order to satisfy the fees of jailers. Hermione, trying to persuade Polixenes, King of Bohemia, to prolong his stay at the court of Leontes in Sicily, says to him, —

> Will you go yet?
> Force me to keep you *as a prisoner,*
> Not like a guest; *so you shall pay your fees*
> *When you depart,* and save your thanks.

Again in "The Third Part of Henry VI.," Act iv. sc. 6, in the scene in the Tower, King Henry inquires of the Lieutenant of the Tower, —

> Master lieutenant, now that God and friends
> Have shaken Edward from the regal seat,
> And turn'd my captive state to liberty,
> My fear to hope, my sorrows unto joys, —
> *At our enlargement what are thy due fees ?*

The Seven Bishops. When the Seven Bishops were brought before the Court of King's Bench by a writ of habeas corpus, on leaving the Tower they refused to pay the fees required by Sir Edward

Hales as lieutenant, whom they charged with discourtesy. He so far forgot himself as to say that the fees were a compensation for the irons with which he might have loaded them, and the bare walls and floor to which he might have confined their accommodation.

" I remember," writes Lord Campbell, "when the Clerk of Assize and the Clerk of the Peace were entitled to exact their fee from all acquitted prisoners, and were supposed in strictness to have a *lien* on their persons for it. I believe there is now no tribunal in England where the practice remains, excepting the two Houses of Parliament; but the Lord Chancellor and the Speaker of the House of Commons still say to prisoners about to be liberated from the custody of the Black Rod or the Sergeant-at-Arms, 'You are discharged, *paying your fees.*'"

Lord Campbell.

In " Love's Labour 's Lost," Act ii. sc. 1, is this passage, which has occasioned some difficulty : —

BOYET. So you grant pasture for me.
[*Offering to kiss her.*
MARIA.   Not so, gentle beast:
My lips are no *common*, though *several* they be.
BOYET. Belonging to whom?
MARIA.   To my fortunes and me.

Shakespeare, vol. iii. p. 453.

Mr. Grant White gives this explanation:
" Maria's meaning and her first pun are plain
enough: the second has been hitherto explained by the statement that the several or
severell in England was a part of the common, set apart for some particular person or
purpose, and that the town bull had equal
right of pasture in common and severell. It
seems to me, however, that we have here another exhibition of Shakespeare's familiarity
with the law; and that the allusion is to ten-
ancy in common by several (i. e. divided, dis-

Co. Litt. lib. iii. cap. 4, sect. 292.

tinct) title. Thus, — ' Tenants in Common
are they which have Lands or Tenements in
Fee-simple, fee-taile, or for terme of life, &c.,
and they have such Lands or Tenements by
severall Titles, and not by a joynt Title, and
none of them know by this his severall, but
they ought by the Law to occupie these

Lands or Tenements in common and *pro indiviso*, to take the profits in Common.' 'Also if lands be given to two to have and to hold s.[everally] the one moiety to the one and to his heires, and the other moiety to the other and to his heires, they are Tenants in Common.' Maria's lips were several as being two, and (as she says in the next line) as belonging in common to her fortunes and to herself; but yet they were no common pasture."

Ib. sect. 298; and see this Chapter *passim.*

" The difficulty in this passage has arisen from the particle *though*, which appears to destroy the antithesis between *common*, i. e. public land, and *several*, which, in the ordinary acceptation, implies enclosed or private property. If, however, we take both as places devoted to pasture, — the one for general, the other for particular use, — the meaning is easy enough. Boyet asks permission to graze on her lips. 'Not so,' she answers; 'my lips, though intended for the purpose, are not for general use.' "

Staunton, Shakespeare, vol. i. p. 86.

" Fields that were enclosed were called *severals*, in opposition to *commons*, the former

Halliwell, vol. iv. p. 274, fol. ed.

belonging to individuals, the others to the inhabitants generally. When commons were enclosed, portions allotted to owners of free-holds, copyholds, and cottages, were fenced in, and termed *severals :* so Maria says, playing on the word, — my lips are not common though they are certainly several, once part of the common ; or, though my lips are several, a field, they are certainly no common. Accord-ing to Mr. Hunter, 'severals, or several lands, are portions of common assigned for a term to a particular proprietor, the other common-ers waiving for the time their right of common over them ;' but, although the term may have been used in this and some other restricted senses, there can be no doubt but that the meaning was generally accepted in accord-ance with the explanation given above."

New Illustra-
tions of Shake-
speare, vol. i.
p. 267.

" My lips are no common, though *several* they be ; " a several is a stinted pasture, or joint possession of a few individuals.

Croft, quoted by
Halliwell, ubi
supra.

> Why should my heart think that a *several* plot
> Which my heart knows the wide world's *common* place ?
> Sonnet CXXXVII.

In " The Comedy of Errors," Act iv. sc. 2,
Shakespeare's knowledge of the language of
pleading, process, and officers, is apparent.
Adriana asks Dromio of Syracuse, " Where
is thy master, Dromio? is he well?" and
Dromio replies, —

No, he's in Tartar limbo, worse than hell.
A devil in an everlasting garment hath him ;
One whose hard heart is button'd up with steel ;
A fiend, a fury, pitiless and rough ;
A wolf, nay, worse, — a fellow all *in buff;*
A back friend, a shoulder-clapper, one that countermands
The passages of alleys, creeks, and narrow lands ;
A hound that runs counter, and yet draws dry foot well;
One that, before the judgment, carries poor souls to hell.

ADR.   Why, man, what is the matter?
DRO. S.   I do not know the matter : he is 'rested
              on *the case.*
ADR.   What, is he arrested? tell me at whose suit.
DRO. S.   I know not at whose suit he is arrested
              well ;
But 'is *in a suit of buff* which 'rested him, that can I tell.
ADR.   This I wonder at,
That he, unknown to me, should be in debt. —
Tell me, was he arrested on a *band?*
DRO. S.   Not on a *band,* but on a stronger thing, —
A chain, a chain.

A sergeant's buff leather garment was called
durance; partly, it would appear, on account

of its *everlasting* qualities, and partly from a quibble on the occupation of the wearer, which was that of arresting and clapping men in *durance* or prison. This peculiar garb is again referred to in a passage in " The First Part of Henry IV.," Act i. sc. 2, —

And is not a *buff* jerkin a most sweet robe of *durance ?*

the point of which seems not to have been fully understood by the commentators. A *robe of durance* was a cant term, implying imprisonment; and the prince, after dilating on purse-stealing, humorously calls attention to its probable consequences, by his query about the *buff jerkin.* See Middleton's " Blurt, Master Constable," Act iii. sc. 2 : —

Tell my lady, that I *go in a suit of durance.*

Staunton, vol. i. p. 204.
To run *counter* is to follow on a false scent : to *draw dry foot* means to track by the mere scent of the foot. A hound that does one is not likely to do the other : but the ambiguity is explained by the double meaning attached to the words *counter* and *dry foot*, — the

former implying both *false* and a *prison ;* and the latter, privation of *scent* and *lack of means.* The sheriff's officer, as he tracks for a prison, may be said to *run counter ;* and, as he follows those who have expended their substance, he *draws dry foot.*

By *before the judgment*, Dromio is supposed to allude to arrest on *mesne process.* *Hell* was a term for the worst dungeon in the wretched prisons of the time. The department thus called was the receptacle of those who had no means to pay the extortionate fines exacted for better accommodation.

Gifford's note to "The City Madam," Act i. sc. i. Vol. 4, p. 7, ed. 1813.

This scene in the fourth act of " The Comedy of Errors " shows that Shakespeare was very familiar with some of the most refined of the principles of the science of special pleading; a science which contains the quintessence of the law. Dromio very correctly answers that his master was arrested in an *action on the case* for the price of a gold chain. " The line drawn by the law between actions on the case and actions of trespass," said

Trespass on the case.

2 W. Bl. 892;
s. c. 1 Smith
L. C. 405, 5th
London ed.

Lord Chief Justice de Grey, in the leading case of Scott *v.* Shepherd, " is very nice and delicate." And although statutes have been passed, both in England and some of the United States, abolishing special demurrers,

See Sharrod *v.*
Railway Co.
4 Exch. 580.

and allowing the joinder of different forms of action, the distinction, often subtle and refined, sometimes invisible, between trespass and case serves in many instances as a test of substantial liability.

Indictment.

In the Court of Justice in " The Winter's Tale," Act iii. sc. 2, the indictment against Queen Hermione for high treason is framed with quite as much technical precision as is now required in England since the passage of Lord Campbell's Act, 14 & 15 Vict. c. 100 : —

Hermione, queen to the worthy Leontes, king of Sicilia, thou art here accused and arraigned of high treason, in committing adultery with Polixenes, king of Bohemia, and conspiring with Camillo to take away the life of our sovereign lord the king, thy royal husband : the pretence whereof being by circumstances partly laid open, thou, Hermione, contrary to the faith and allegiance of a true subject, didst counsel and aid them, for their better safety, to fly away by night.

And the same remark applies to the indictment on which Lord Say was arraigned: —

Thou hast most traitorously corrupted the youth of the realm in erecting a grammar-school: and whereas, before, our forefathers had no other books but the score and the tally, thou hast caused printing to be used ; and, *contrary to the king, his crown, and dignity*, thou hast built a paper-mill. It will be proved to thy face that thou hast men about thee that usually talk of a noun and a verb, *and such abominable words as no Christian ear can endure to hear.* Thou hast appointed justices of peace, to call poor men before them about matters they were not able to answer. Moreover, thou hast put them in prison ; *and because they could not read, thou hast hanged them ; when, indeed, only for that cause they have been most worthy to live.*

Henry VI. Part II. Act iv. sc. 7.

3 Inst. 59.

At the period when Shakespeare wrote, whilst persons, to their destruction, were presumed to be learned in point of *law*, they were customarily hanged by reason of ignorance, in point of *fact*, depriving them of the benefit of clergy. As Cade says, —

Thou hast put men in prison ; and because they could not read, thou hast hanged them ; when, indeed, only for that cause they have been most worthy to live.

Cade's proclamation, announcing the policy he should pursue during his administration, alludes to an ancient feudal custom : —

Henry VI. Part II. Act iv. sc. 7. The proudest peer in the realm shall not wear a head on his shoulders, unless he pay me tribute ; *there shall not a maid be married, but she shall pay to me her maidenhead ere they have it:* men shall hold of me *in capite ;* and we charge and command that their wives be *as free as heart can wish or tongue can tell.*

The lord of the fee had anciently a right to lie with his tenant's wife on her wedding night. Cade declares his intention to assume this right, "with this alteration, that instead of conferring the privilege on every lord of a manor, to be exercised within the manor, he is to assume it exclusively for himself all over the realm, as belonging to his prerogative royal;" imitating, in this respect, the custom of one of the nations of Libyans (as related by Herodotus), who exhibited to the king their virgins who were about to marry; and, if any one suited the pleasure of his majesty, he deflowered her.

Cade then proceeds to announce, as a part of the policy of his government, that he shall abolish tenure in *free socage* and that all *men* shall hold of him *in capite;* and, although his subjects should no longer hold in free socage, "their wives should be as free as heart can wish or tongue can tell." Strange to say, says Lord Campbell, this phrase, or one almost identically the same, "as free as tongue can speak or heart can think," is feudal, and was known to the ancient law of England. In the tenth year of King Henry VII., Lord Chief Justice Hussey, in a considered judgment, delivered the opinion of the whole Court of King's Bench as to the construction to be put upon the words, "as free as tongue can speak or heart can think."

Melpom. iv. 168.

Lord Campbell.

Year Book, Hil. Term, 10 Hen. VII. fol. 13, pl. 6.

Absque hoc.

Stephen Pl. 193-
218, 5th ed.
9 A. & E. 309.

In " The Second Part of Henry IV.," Act v. sc. 5, Pistol uses the term, *absque hoc*, which is technical in the last degree. This was a species of traverse, used by special pleaders when the record was in Latin, known by the denomination of a *special traverse*. The subtlety of its texture, and the total dearth of explanation in all the Reports and treatises extant in the time of Shakespeare with respect to its principle, seem to justify the conclusion that he must have attained a knowledge of it from actual practice.

The Reporters,
pp. 147-153,
4th ed.

The first scene in the fifth act of " Hamlet " " is the mine which has produced the richest legal ore." I print from " The Reporters " Mr. Wallace's entertaining version of this scene, and of the legal and logical subtleties involved in the celebrated case of

1 Plowd. 253.

Hales *v.* Petit reported in Plowden's Commentaries, the arguments and decision in which it has been suggested that Shakespeare intended to ridicule.

It has been supposed by a very grave writer, at once a lawyer and a critic, and, indeed, has been very extensively believed, that Hales *v*. Petit, one of Plowden's cases, furnished to Shakespeare part of the scene of the grave-diggers in Hamlet. Whether, as it has been thus supposed, Shakespeare ever studied the Reports of Plowden, then still in Norman French, or whether only in the pervading ubiquity and power of his genius, he was uttering, in the unreal dialogue of clowns, the actual language of ermined nonsense, may not now be easy to decide. For myself, I should rather recall the suggestions of Gibbon, who, noting some beautiful lines of Gregory Nazianzen, which burst from the heart and speak the pangs of injured and lost friendship, directs attention to the coincidence of phraseology in these and the pathetic complaint which Helena in " The Midsummer Night's Dream " addresses to her friend, Hermia, upon the same subject. " Shakespeare," he adds, however, " had never read the poems of Gregory Nazianzen: he

Sir John Hawkins, note to Hamlet, Act v. sc. 1. " The New Variorum," vol. iii. p. 376 note.

Decline and Fall, chapter xxvii., A. D. 340, 380.

was ignorant of the Greek language; but his mother-tongue, the language of Nature, is the same in Cappadocia and in Britain." Whether Shakespeare studied Plowden or not, his grave-diggers in Hamlet, it is certain, have left a satire on the "sober follies" of the court, by arguments so like their own as to have originated the conjecture that "Decisions in Westminster" must have been transcribed for the entertainment of groundlings at the "Globe Theatre" and "Blackfriars." The case was thus:—

The Reporters, p. 148, 4th ed.

Sir James Hales, one of the Justices of Common Pleas, and the son of Sir John Hales, eminent as a Baron of the Exchequer, had committed suicide, in his sober senses, by drowning himself in a river or watercourse near his house in Canterbury. The coroner, with his jury, sat upon the body, and presented that "passing through ways and streets in the same city unto the aforesaid river," Sir James had "voluntarily entered the same, and himself therein feloniously and voluntarily drowned." A lease to him and

his wife as *joint tenants* was seized by the
Crown as forfeited by the felony of his suicide, and re-granted to Petit, who endeavored
to enter, while Lady Hales, claiming as sur-
vivor in joint-tenancy to her lord, sued Petit
for the trespass. It being admitted that if
Sir James had committed felony in his lifetime, the lease was forfeited, the question
before the court was, whether Sir James, in
drowning himself, had committed suicide in
his own lifetime. For if the felony was not
committed until after he was dead, then Lady
Hales clearly had the case.

A Justice of the King's court — himself a
son of one of the King's Barons of the Exchequer — charged with having committed
a felony when alive, was an allegation not
common in Westminster Hall, and to have
committed the offence after he was dead was
an imputation still more alarming; while to
have achieved any such misfortune in the
imaginary instant of "betweenity"— that is
to say, when he was neither dead *nor* alive —
was as difficult of comprehension as either of

the other possibilities. The *experimentum in corpore vili* was a reproach which no one could throw upon the counsel. It was clearly a great case. Six sergeants-at-law argued it, and their dialectics would have done honor to all the monks that ever assembled round the cell or the shrine of the saint of Canterbury himself.

The Reporters,
149, 4th ed.

Lady Hales' counsel contended that, to make the felony, both the cause of the death and the death itself must unite and be complete. "A man could not be *felo de se* until the death of himself be fully had and consummate." The death must precede the felony, and *à fortiori*, the forfeiture, which was its consequence. Here, admitting that the cause of his death — the throwing himself into the water — was done in his lifetime, and so completed, still, the death was a thing subsequent, and not complete in his lifetime. When he was dead he was not alive. The death was not to have relation to the cause of it, as was shown by a position assumed as admitted, that if A. gave B. a mortal stab, of which B. died, only some time after, A. might give away his goods to C. after the stab, and before the death, and the gift would be good ; and by a case cited from 11 Henry IV., where Year Book, 11 Hen. IV. two constables had voluntarily let a man escape that had given a wound to another, who afterwards died of it ; yet it was not felony in the constables, "for the death hath no relation to the cause of it, nor was he that gave the wound a felon before the party dieth." Although "the forfeiture comes at the same instant that he dies, yet in things of an instant there is a priority of time in consideration of law, and the one shall be said to precede the other, although both shall be said to happen at one instant, for every instant contains the end of one time and the commencement of another. And accordingly here the death and the forfeiture shall come together, and at one same time, and yet there is a priority, that is, the end of his life makes the commencement of the forfeiture, though, at the same time, the forfeiture is so near to the death, that there is no mean time between

them, yet notwithstanding that, in consideration of law, the one precedes the other, but by
no means has the forfeiture relation to any
time in his life."

The Reporters,
p. 150, 4th ed.

This clear and lucid explanation of the
whole matter it was not easy to answer; and
four sergeants, Walsh, Comly, Benloe, and
Carus, argued *e contra* for Petit. · They contended that the forfeiture was to have relation to the act done in the party's lifetime,
which was the cause of his death, and upon
this that the parts of the act were to be considered. " And Walsh said, that the act
consists of three parts. The first is the im-
agination, which is a reflection or meditation
of the mind, whether or no it is convenient
for him to destroy himself, and what way it
can be done. The second is the resolution,
which is a determination of the mind to destroy himself, and to do it in this or that particular way. The third is the perfection,
which is the execution of what the mind has
resolved to do. And this perfection consists
of two parts; viz., the beginning and the end.

The beginning is the doing of the act which causes the death, and the end is the death, which is only a sequel to the act."

These elementary divisions were amplified and complicated in a style worthy of their conception, and until the matter was fairly twisted and knotted into a state fit for the judicial explication.

The Reporters, p. 150, 4th ed.

In giving judgment upon their late brother, " the Lord Dyer said, that *five* things were to be considered in the case, —

1. The quality of the offence of Sir James Hales ;
2. To whom the offence is committed ;
3. What shall he forfeit ?
4. From what time the forfeiture shall commence ; and
5. If the term here shall be taken from the wife."

On the 1st point, it was clear that Sir James had been acting by the instigation of the devil, and was a murderer.

On the 2d, that as the king, as head, " had lost one of his mystical members," the offence was against *him*.

On the 3d, that his majesty, having the right to the goods of felons, on account of the loss he suffered in their death, and "not in respect that holy church will not meddle with them," was entitled to Sir James's goods.

The Reporters, p. 151, 4th ed.

But the great point of difficulty, the 4th point, — that is to say, whether the Right Honorable Justice, who had so lately drowned himself, had done so while he was alive, — seems to have been settled conclusively by Sir Anthony Browne. "He said Sir James Hales was dead; and how came he to his death? It may be answered, by drowning. And who drowned him? Sir James Hales. And when did he drown him? In his life time. So that Sir James Hales, being alive, caused Sir James Hales to die; and the act of the living man was the death of the dead man. And then for this offence it is reasonable to punish the living man who committed the offence, and not the dead man. But how can he be said to be punished alive, when the punishment comes after his death? Sir, this can be done no other way but by divesting out of him, from the time of the act done in his life, which was the cause of his death, the title and property of those things which he had in his lifetime."

The judicial duty which was included in this case of Hales *v.* Petit, it must be confessed, was a hard one. It seems, in fact, to have involved the necessity of finding the dividing line between To be and Not to be; to discern, to catch, and to fix an object which lies between substance and thin air; — to retain the bubble in its act of bursting. It was, in truth, the very question with which Lorenzo de Medici, when descending from magnificence to waggery, puzzled, A. D. 1490, the learned Salviati, and which that astute theologian, replying to his patron, thought worthy of an entire treatise learnedly composed in the language of scholars, and divided into no less than seven parts; a volume yet preserved among the treasures of the Laurentian Library at Florence, where, during two years that I passed in that beautiful city, I often resorted to be entertained by

Roscoe, Life of Lorenzo de Medici, p. 294, 10th ed. London, 1851.

The Reporters,
p. 152, 4th ed.

its treasures of manuscript lore. " If no man,"
said Lorenzo to his ghostly father, " can effec-
tually exert himself to obtain eternal happi-
ness without the special favor of God, and if
that favor be only granted to those who are
well disposed towards the reception, I wish
to know whether the grace of God or the
good disposition first commences." The so-
lution which Salviati gave his reverent pupil
may yet be seen. It was worthy of all that
Sir Anthony Browne urged against the case
of Lady Hales, or that any other of the judges
argued in its behalf. And if the Italian had
only been dressed in the judicial ermine and
a wig, instead of in the sacerdotal cassock
and *calotte*, he would undoubtedly have ex-
ceeded every one who "argued." His logic
and his learning was even superior to theirs.

William Shakespeare, however, to whom
the main case — that, we mean, of Hales *v.*
Petit — came on for final judgment, placed it
on grounds not touched by the sergeants or
the court, and which even the subtle Floren-
tine does not adumbrate. *His* argument is,

that as the water was running water, and came down stream, the unfortunate *felo de se* did not drown himself at all: the water drowned him. Here is his view of it :—

FIRST CLOWN. It must be *se offendendo;* it cannot be else. For here lies the point : if I drown myself wittingly, it argues an act : and an act hath three branches; it is, to act, to do, to perform : argal, she drowned herself wittingly.

SECOND CLOWN. Nay, but hear you, goodman delver, —

FIRST CLOWN. Give me leave. Here lies the water ; good : here stands the man ; good : if the man go to this water and drown himself, it is, will he, nill he, he goes, — mark you that; but if the water come to him and drown him, he drowns not himself: argal, he that is not guilty of his own death shortens not his own life.

SECOND CLOWN. But is this law?

FIRST CLOWN. Ay, marry is 't ; crowner's quest-law.

The whole discussion in Plowden must submit itself to the superior wisdom of Shakespeare's clowns ; especially as evidence still preserved would indicate that Sir James did not destroy himself at all, but that his death

See Foss, Judges of England, vol. v. p. 373.

"was occasioned by his crossing a river over a narrow bridge from which he *accidentally* fell and was drowned," at the immature age of eighty-five.

Overseers in wills.

Overseers were frequently added in wills, says Malone, from the superabundant caution of our ancestors; but the law acknowledges no such persons, nor are they (as contradistinguished from executors) invested with any legal right whatever. In some old wills the term *overseer* is used instead of executor.

> Thou, Collatine, shalt *oversee this will.*
> *The Rape of Lucrece.*

It is noticeable that Shakespeare, in his own will, appoints John Hall, his son-in-law, and Susanna, his eldest daughter, executors; and Thomas Hall and Francis Collins *overseers.*

Statutes.

In the following sentence, the word "statutes" is used in a sense purely technical: —

This fellow might be in's time a great buyer of land, with his *statutes*, his recognizances, his fines, his double vouchers, his recoveries. — *Hamlet*, Act v. sc. I.

In Sonnet CXXXIV. the word *statute* has also its legal signification, that of a security or obligation for money : —

> The *statute* of thy beauty thou wilt take.

The statutes here referred to are not Acts of Parliament, but statutes merchant and statutes staple.   Both the statute merchant and statute staple are securities for money; the one entered into before the chief magistrate of some trading town, pursuant to the statute 13 Edw. I. " De Mercatoribus," and thence called a statute merchant ; the other pursuant to the statute Edw. III. c. 9, before the mayor of the staple, that is to say, the grand mart for the principal commodities or manufactures of the kingdom, formerly held by Act of Parliament in certain trading towns, from whence this security is called a statute staple. Thus, in Lilly's " Mother Bombie : " —

2 Bl. Comm. 160.

" Mother
Bombie."

HALF. I'le enter into a statute marchant to see
it answered. But if thou wilt have bonds, thou
shalt have a bushell full.

HACK. Alas, poore ant! thou bound in a statute marchant? a browne threed will binde thee fast
enough : but if you will be content all foure joyntly
to enter into a bond, I will withdraw the action. —
Act iv. sc. 2, vol. ii. p. 129, ed. Fairholt.

" The Family
of Love."

In Middleton's " The Family of Love," Glis-
ter says, —

Tut, you are master Dryfat the merchant ; your
skill is greater in cony-skins and wool packs than
in gentlemen. His lands be in *statutes:* you mer-
chants were wont to be *merchant staplers;* but now
gentlemen have gotten up the trade, for there is
not one gentleman amongst twenty but his land[s]
be engaged in twenty *statutes staple.* — Act i. sc. 3,
vol. ii. p. 123, ed. Dyce.

"Censura Lit-
eraria," vol.
vii. p. 16, 1st ed.

In Nash's " Pierce Penilesse," 1592, is this
passage : —

I was informed of late daies, that a certayne
blind retayler called the Divell, used to lend money
upon pawnes, or any thing, and would let one for a
need have a thousand poundes upon a *statute merchant* of his soule.

3 Bl. Comm. 419.

In the case of recognizances or debts acknowledged on statutes merchant or statutes staple, pursuant to the statutes 13 Edw. I. "De Mercatoribus," and 27 Edw. III. c. 9, upon forfeiture of these, the body, lands, and goods may all be taken at once in execution to compel the payment of the debt. The process hereon is called an *extent*, or *extendi facias*, because the sheriff is to cause the lands, &c. to be appraised to their full *extended* value before he delivers them to the person entitled under a recognizance, &c. that it may be certainly known how soon the debt will be satisfied. In the old dramatists, the word is constantly used in its legal sense. Lord Campbell quotes the following passage as an example of Shakespeare's "deep technical knowledge of the law:" —

> DUKE FRED. Well, push him out of doors ;
> And let my officers of such a nature
> *Make an extent upon his house and lands.*
> > *As You Like It*, Act iii. sc. 1.

They are usurers, they come yawning for money ; and the sheriff with them is come to serve an *extent upon your land* and then seize on your body by force of execution. — *The Miseries of Inforced Marriage*, Act v. DODSLEY'S *Old Plays*, vol. v. p. 96, ed. 1780.

> Mark me ; widows
> Are long *extents* in law upon men's livings,
> Upon their bodies' winding-sheets ; they that enjoy 'em
> Lie with but dead men's monuments, and beget
> Only their own ill epitaphs.
>
> FLETCHER'S *Wit Without Money*, Act ii. sc. 2.

> When
> This *manor is extended* to my use,
> You 'll speak in an humbler key, and sue for favor.
>
> MASSINGER'S *A New Way to Pay Old Debts*, Act v. sc. 1.

Nieces, my *land* in the country is *extended*, and my goods seiz'd on. — SHADWELL'S *The Virtuoso*, Act. v. p. 61, ed. 1691.

> If that shepherd be not in *hand-fast*, let him fly.
>
> *The Winter's Tale*, Act iv. sc. 3.

Staunton, vol. iii. p. 776.

To be in "hand-fast" = *mainprize*, is to be at large on security given. Sometimes this state was called *handling*. Thus, in "The London Prodigal," Act iii. sc. 3: "Ay, but he is now in hucster's *handling* for (i. e. for fear of) running away." Of the writ of main-prize nothing is now known in practice. The distinction between mainpernors and bail was technical and well defined in the time of Shakespeare.

The phrase in "A Midsummer Night's Dream," Act i. sc. 1, —

> according to our law
> Immediately provided in that case,

would stand the test of general professional observation at the present day.

The two great disposing powers of transfer of land, in the primitive ages of the common law, were Feoffment and Grant. A feoffment carried destruction in its course by operating upon the possession, without any regard to the interest or estate of the feoffer. Thus, when Henry IV. says that Richard

> *Enfeoff'd himself* to popularity,

he means that he gave himself up absolutely to popularity.

Henry IV. Part I. Act iii. sc. 2.

The practice of using the written examinations of absent witnesses, instead of their vivâ voce evidence in the presence of the prisoner, is alluded to in "Henry the Eighth," Act ii. sc. 1, in the passage which gives the account of the trial of the Duke of Buckingham, who was convicted and executed for saying, "If the king should arrest him of high treason, he would stab the king with his dagger."

Owen alias Collins's Case, Godbolt, pl. 363, p. 264.

> The great duke
> Came to the bar; where to his accusations
> He pleaded still, not guilty, and alleg'd
> Many sharp reasons to defeat the law.
> The king's attorney, on the contrary,
> Urg'd on th' examinations, proofs, confessions
> Of divers witnesses; which the duke desired
> To have brought vivâ voce, to his face.

The evidence of verbal confessions of guilt is to be received with great caution. Macaulay has expressed this rule in forcible language. "Words," says he, "may easily be misunderstood by an honest man. They may easily be misconstrued by a knave. What was spoken metaphorically may be apprehended

History of England, vol. i. ch. 5.

seriously. A particle, a tense, a mood, an emphasis, may make the whole difference between guilt and innocence."

In "The Merchant of Venice," Antonio's bond to Shylock is prepared and talked about according to the forms observed in an English attorney's office. The distinction is observed between a *single* bond, a *simplex obligatio,* and a bond with a *condition.* Shylock says, —

> Go with me to a notary, seal me there
> Your *single* bond. Act i. sc. 3.

On the forfeiture of a conditional bond, the whole penalty, which is usually double the principal sum, was recoverable at law. Thus, in "Venus and Adonis," —

> Say, for non-payment that the debt should *double.*

But here the courts of equity interposed, and would not permit a party to take more than in conscience he ought. In the famous trial in the first scene of the fourth act of "The

Lord Campbell.

Bond.

Merchant of Venice," Bassanio, counsel for the defendant, beseeches the fair judge not to maintain this rigid rule of law, inaccessible to the dictates and appeal of equity : —

> BASS.   And I beseech you,
> Wrest once the law to your authority :
> To do a great right, do a little wrong ;
> And curb this cruel devil of his will.
>   PORTIA.   It must not be ; there is no power in Venice
> Can alter a decree establishèd :
> *'Twill be recorded for a precedent ;*
> And many an error, by the same example,
> Will rush into the State : it cannot be.
>
>   .   .   .   .
>
>   Why, this bond is forfeit ;
> And lawfully by this the Jew may claim
> A pound of flesh, to be by him cut off
> Nearest the merchant's heart.

In " The Taming of the Shrew," Induction, sc. 2, a servant says to Sly, —

> For though you lay here in this goodly chamber,
> Yet would you say, ye were beaten out of door ;
> And rail upon the hostess of the house ;
> And say, you would *present her at the Leet,*
> *Because she brought stone jugs and no seal'd quarts.*

Shakespeare evinces a knowledge of the juris-
diction of the Court Leet, in his time, the
lowest court of criminal judicature in England. In this court, parties in the practice of
using false weights and measures were pre-
sentable and punishable. The *sealed quarts*
were the licensed quart measures, certified by
stamp to be capable of holding that quantity
of liquid. Malone cites the following pas-
sage from Lenton's " Leasures " (1631) : —

He [an informer] transforms himselfe into several shapes, to avoid suspicion of *inneholders*, and
inwardly joyes at the sight of a blacke pot or *jugge*,
knowing that their sale by *sealed quarts* spoyles
his market.

The Court of Wards was first erected in
Henry the Eighth's time, and was afterwards
augmented by him with the office of liveries;
hence called the Court of Wards and Liveries. Under the feudal system, every estate
was considered as a benefice, which, while the
heir was a minor, or otherwise incapable of
serving, reverted to the superior, who ap-

pointed another to perform military service in his stead. While this prerogative remained, the king, as feudal superior, gave or sold the wardship of a minor to whomsoever he chose, with as much of the income as he thought proper. *If the heir was a female, the king was entitled to offer her any husband of her rank, at his option; and, if she refused him, she forfeited her land.*

Shakespeare, who gives to all nations the customs of his own, in a passage in " The Comedy of Errors," Act v. sc. 1, alludes to a Court of Wards at Ephesus. Adriana addresses the duke : —

> May 't please your grace, Antipholus my husband, —
> *Who I made lord of me and all I had,*
> *At your important letters.*

In this passage Shakespeare was thinking particularly on the interest which the king in England had in the marriage of his wards, — an interest which Queen Elizabeth in Shakespeare's time exerted on all occasions, as did her successors, till the abolition of the

Court of Wards and Liveries by statute 12 Car. II.

The Court of Wards was always considered as a grievous oppression. The abuse above spoken of is distinctly alluded to in Ben Jonson's "Bartholomew Fair." Grace Wellborn, being asked how she came under the guardianship of Justice Overdo, replies,—

" Bartholomew Fair."

Faith, through a common calamity, he bought me, sir; and now *he will marry me to his wife's brother*, this wise gentleman that you see; *or else I must pay value o' my land.* — Act iii. sc. 1, vol. iv. p. 459, ed. Gifford.

See Massinger's "The Guardian," Act i. sc. 1, vol. iv. p. 125, ed. Gifford (1805).

Peine forte et dure was a punishment, by which a prisoner indicted for felony was compelled to put himself upon his trial. If, when arraigned, he stood mute, he was remanded to prison, and placed in a low dark chamber, and there laid on his back on the bare floor naked, unless when decency forbade; upon his body was placed as great a weight of iron as he could bear; on the first day he received

Peine forte et dure.

4 Bl. Comm. 325. Stephen Hist. Crim. Law of England, vol. i. p. 298.

no sustenance, save three morsels of the worst bread, and on the second day three draughts of standing water that should be nearest to the prison-door, and such was alternately his daily diet till he pleaded or died. This punishment was vulgarly called *pressing to death*. In " Much Ado About Nothing," Act iii. sc. 1, Hero says of Beatrice, —

> If I should speak,
> She 'd mock me into air ; O, she would laugh me
> Out of myself, *press me to death* with wit !

In " King Richard II." Act iii. sc. 4, in the scene in the garden, the Queen exclaims, " O, I am press'd to death through want of speaking !"   And in " Troilus and Cressida," Act iii. sc. 2, Pandarus says to Cressida, " I will show you a chamber with a bed ; which bed, because it shall not speak of your pretty encounters, press it to death."   The Queen and Pandarus refer not only to this punishment, but also to its cause, namely, " refusing to speak," or, " standing mute " or, in the Queen's own words, " want of speaking."

Year Books,
30 and 31 Edw. I.

In Appendix I. to " Year Books," 30 and 31 Edward I. p. 510, is this case : —

John de Dorley was arraigned for divers felonies ; and he stood mute, and would not speak a word. The Justice inquired if he was dumb, or if he could speak if he chose. The inquest said he could speak if he chose. And because he would not put himself on the country, or answer, he was adjudged to suffer penance ; namely, that he should be put in a house on the ground in his shirt, laden with as much iron as he could bear, and that he should have nothing to drink on the day when he had any thing to eat, and that he should drink water which came neither from fountain nor river. The same penance was adjudged to Sir Ralph Bloyho, because he would not put himself on the country.

The invitation of Pointz, in " The First Part of King Henry IV." Act i. sc. 2, to " my lads," to an excursion to Gadshill, which was notorious for the robberies committed there, recalls a singular case in Leonard, who reported decisions contemporaneously with Shakespeare, where a Hundred, against

2 Leonard, 12.

whom an action had been brought for a robbery, pleaded "that time out of mind felons had used to rob at Gadshill, and so prescribed."

Taken with the manner.

The phrase, "taken with the manner," occurs in Shakespeare. It means to be caught in a criminal act; originally in a theft, with the thing stolen in hand. Cowel thus explains it: "*Mainour*, alias *manour*, alias *meinour*, from the French *manier*, i. e. *manu tractare*: in a legal sense denotes the thing that a thief taketh or stealeth; as to be taken with the *mainour* is to be taken with the thing stolen about him." In "Pleas of the Crown before Spigurnel, &c." published in Appendix I. to "Year Books," 30 and 31 Edward I. p. 512, is the following case, decided in 1302:—

Cowel, Law Dict. *s. v.* "Mainour."

Year Books, 30 and 31 Edw. I.

If a thief be taken with the "mainour," with oxen or other chattels, and the owner of the chattels pursue the thief, and the thief abandon the oxen or the chattels, and the bailiff of the liberty take them, and assign a day to the owner, and receive his proof of ownership of the chattels, and deliver to him the chattels (as it happened to the sheriff of Cornwall regarding two oxen which were delivered in that manner), he shall be charged with them, and shall answer to the king.

The phrase also occurs in the translation of the Bible of 1611 : —

Bible, 1611.

If any man's wife go aside, and commit a trespass against him, and a man lie with her carnally, and it be hid from the eyes of her husband, and be kept close, and she be defiled, and *there be* no witness against her, neither she be *taken with the manner.* — Numb. v. 12, 13.

In "The First Part of Henry IV." Prince Henry exclaims, —

O villain, thou stolest a cup of sack eighteen years ago, and wert *taken with the manner.* — Act ii. sc. 4.

In "Love's Labour's Lost," Act i. sc. 1, Costard quibbles on *manner*, i.e. the thing stolen, and *manor*, house, where he was arrested.

COSTARD. The matter is to me, sir, as concerning Jaquenetta. The manner of it is, I was taken *with the manner.*

BIRON. In what manner?

COST. In manner and form following, sir; all those three: I was seen with her in the manor-house, sitting with her upon the form, and taken following her into the park; which, put together, is in manner and form following. Now, sir, for the manner, — it is the manner of a man to speak to a woman: for the form, — in some form.

The expression, "taken yourself with the manner," occurs in the third scene of the fourth act of "The Winter's Tale." "*With* the manner" is more proper than "*in* the manner;" and accordingly Latimer writes correctly, —

Even as a theife that is taken, *with the maner* that he stealeth. — *Sermons*, 110.

Subornation of perjury.

In "Othello," Desdemona says, —

Beshrew me much, Emilia,
I was — unhandsome warrior as I am —
Arraigning his unkindness with my soul;
But now I find I had *suborn'd the witness*,
And he's indicted falsely.   Act iii. sc. 4.

This is clearly a reference to the crime of subornation of perjury, which is an offence at common law, and consists in the procuring another to take such a false oath as constitutes perjury in the principal, or person taking it.

As has already been observed, the gravediggers' scene in Hamlet " is the mine which produces the richest legal ore." Lord Campbell remarks: " These terms of art are all used seemingly with a full knowledge of their import; and it would puzzle some practising barristers with whom I am acquainted to go over the whole *seriatim*, and to define each of them satisfactorily : " —

Hamlet, Act. v.
sc. 1.
Ante, p. 48.

Lord Campbell.

HAMLET. There's another : why might not that be the skull of a lawyer ? Where be his quiddets now, his *quillets*, his *cases*, his *tenures*, and his tricks ? why does he suffer this rude knave now to knock him about the sconce with a dirty shovel, and will not tell him of his *action of battery ?* Hum ! This fellow might be in 's time a great buyer of land, with his *statutes*, his *recognizances*, his *fines*, his *double vouchers*, his *recoveries :* is this the *fine* of his *fines*, and the *recovery* of his *recoveries*, to have his fine pate full of fine dirt ? will his *vouchers* vouch him no more of his *purchases*, and *double ones* too, than the length and breadth of a pair of *indentures?* The very *conveyances* of his lands will hardly lie in this box; and must the *inheritor* himself have no more, ha?

Sonnet XLVI.

Sonnet XLVI. is purely legal both in thought and in expression: —

Mine eye and heart are at a mortal war,
How to divide the conquest of thy sight;
Mine eye my heart thy picture's sight would bar,
My heart mine eye the freedom of that right.
My heart doth plead that thou in him dost lie, —
A closet never pierc'd with crystal eyes, —
But the defendant doth that plea deny,
And says in him thy fair appearance lies.
To cide this title is impannellèd
A quest of thoughts, all tenants to the heart;
And by their verdict is determinèd
The dear eye's moiety and the dear heart's part:
  As thus, — mine eye's due is thy outward part,
  And my heart's right thy inward love of heart.

Lord Campbell.

Lord Campbell well observes, that "even where Shakespeare is most solemn and sublime, his sentiments and language seem some-

times to take a tinge from his early pursuits;"
and cites that splendid passage, in "Measure
for Measure," where Isabella thus speaks to
Angelo, the wicked lord deputy:—

"Measure for Measure," Act ii. sc. 2.

> ANG.   Your brother is a forfeit of the law,
> And you but waste your words.
> ISAB.   Alas, alas!
> Why, all the souls that were were forfeit once;
> And He that might the vantage best have took
> Found out the remedy.   How would you be,
> *If He, which is the top of judgment*, should
> But judge you as you are?   O, think on that;
> And mercy then will breathe within your lips,
> Like man new-made.   Act ii. sc. 2.

Dante, Purgatorio, c. vi. 37.

With equal beauty and propriety, Queen
Katharine, looking to the just judgment of
God, thus addresses the two cardinals:—

> Is this your Christian counsel? out upon ye!
> *Heaven is above all yet; there sits a Judge*
> *That no king can corrupt.*
>   *Henry VIII.* Act iii. sc. 1.

A corresponding sentiment is put by Sophocles with great effect into the mouth of the
Chorus addressing Electra:—

Sophocles.

Θάρσει μοι, θάρσει, τέκνον.
ἔτι μέγας οὐρανῷ
Ζεύς, ὃς ἐφορᾷ πάντα καὶ κρατύνει.

Elect. 173-5.

Choate.

Choate, in an eloquent passage, describing "the good judge," who will not respect persons in judgment, and whose only duty is to attend to the "trepidations of the balance," says: "If Athens comes there to demand that the cup of hemlock be put to the lips of the wisest of men; and he believes that he has not *corrupted the youth, nor omitted to worship the gods of the city, nor introduced new divinities of his own,* he must deliver him, although the thunder light on the unterrified brow."

Countenance.

ROSENCRANTZ. Take you me for a sponge, my lord?

HAMLET. Ay, sir; that soaks up the king's *countenance,* his rewards, his authorities.— *Hamlet,* Act. iv. sc. 2.

"Every Man out of his Humour," Act iii. sc. 1.

SOGLIARDO. You will not serve me, sir, will you? I'll give you more than *countenance.*

BEN JONSON. *Every Man Out of his Humour,* Act iii. sc. 1.

Countenance is a law term from the French *contenement,* or the Latin *contenementum,* and denotes the credit and reputation which a person hath by reason of his freehold; and most commonly what is necessary for his support and maintenance, according to his condition of life.

Barrington, "Observations on the Statutes," p. 11, 5th ed.

Come sit thou here, most learned *justicer.*
King Lear, Act iii. sc. 6.

Justicer.

The most ancient law-books have *justicers* of the peace as frequently as *justices* of the peace. Thus in Lambard's "Eirenarcha," ed. 1582, p. 4: "And of this it commeth that M. Fitzherbert (in his treatise of the Justices of the Peace) calleth them *Justicers* (contractly for *Justiciars*) and not *Justices,* as we commonly, (and not altogether unproperly) do name them."

"Eirenarcha."

In Julius Cæsar, Act i. sc. 3, Casca says:—

My *answer* must be made.

Answer.

"Julius Cæsar,"
p. 114, Claren-
don Press ed.

I shall be called to account, and must answer as for seditious words. In this legal sense "answer" is used in "Henry V." Act ii. sc. 2. : —

> Their faults are open :
> *Arrest* them to the *answer* of the law.

PAROLLES. Sir, for a quart d'écu he will sell the fee-simple of his salvation, the inheritance of it ; and cut the entail from all remainders, and a perpetual succession for it perpetually. — *All's Well that Ends Well*, Act iv. sc. 3.

The idea here intended to be conveyed is clear; but the legal phraseology is nonsensical. The reference is to an estate held in fee, in tail, and in mortmain.

" Pray in aid."

> A conqueror that will *pray in aid* for kindness,
> Where he for grace is kneel'd to.
> > *Antony and Cleopatra*, Act. v. sc. 2.

Hanmer.

Praying in aid is a law term used for a petition made in a court of justice for the calling in of help from another that hath an interest in the cause in question.

In divine learning, we see how frequent parables and tropes are : for it is a rule, that whatsoever science is not consonant to pre-suppositions, must *pray in aid* of similitudes. — BACON, *Advancement of Learning*, II. 17, § 10.

In " Twelfth Night," Act iii. sc. 2, Fabian says to Sir Toby Belch, —

I will prove it legitimate, sir, *upon the oaths* of judgment and reason.

SIR TOBY.   And they have been *grand jury-men* since before Noah was a sailor.

Portia addressing Shylock, —

it appears, by manifest proceeding,
That indirectly, and directly too,
Thou hast contriv'd against the very life
Of the defendant ; and thou hast incurr'd
The danger *formerly* by me rehears'd.
The Merchant of Venice, Act iv. sc. 1.

" Formerly," says Mr. Wright, " was used in legal documents for ' above,' as in the following extract from Sir Robert Hitcham's Will : ' And if the said college shall wilfully refuse

Bacon.

Formerly.

"The Merchant of Venice," Clarendon Press ed. p. 122.

to perform this my will: Then, I will, that
this my Devise unto them shall be void ; and
I do Devise the same unto Emanuel College,
in Cambridge, in the same manner and form,
as it is *formerly* devised unto Pembroke-
Hall, and to the same Uses, Intents, Trusts,
and Purposes.'"— LODER, *Hist. of Framling-
ham*, p. 207.

In " The Comedy of Errors," Act ii. sc. 2,
in the dialogue between Antipholus of Syracuse and his attendant Dromio, is this passage : —

DRO. S.   There's no time for a man to *recover*
his hair that grows bald by nature.

ANT. S.   May he not do it by *fine and recovery ?*

DRO. S.   Yes, to pay a *fine* for a periwig, and
recover the lost hair of another man.

In " The Merry Wives of Windsor," Act
iv. sc. 2, the merry wives, after Falstaff's
experiment upon their virtue, indulge in a

*Fine and
Recovery.*

conversation in which the recondite terms of the law of real property are used with technical precision.

MRS. FORD. What think you? may we, with the *warrant* of womanhood and the *witness* of a good conscience, pursue him with any further revenge?

MRS. PAGE. The spirit of wantonness is, sure, scared out of him : if the devil have him not in *fee simple*, with *fine and recovery*, he will never, I think, in the way of *waste*, attempt us again.

Warrant.

Witness.

" Fee simple, feodum simplex, is that of which we are seized in these general words, To us and our heirs forever." "Fine and recovery " is the strongest assurance known to English law ; and "waste " is any spoil or destruction in houses, gardens, trees, &c., to the prejudice of the heir expectant.

Fee simple.
Cowel Law Dict.
s. v. " Fee,"
ed. 1727.

Ritson.

Waste

But I 'll *amerce* you with so strong a fine,
That you shall all repent the loss of mine.
Romeo and Juliet, Act iii. sc. 1.

Amerce.

In " Paradise Lost," Bk. i. 609, 610, is the expression, " *amerced* of Heaven," i. e. " pun-

Paradise Lost.

ished with the loss of Heaven." The verb " to *amerce* " (noun *amercement* or *amercia-* *ment*) is an old law term, meaning " to punish by a fine at the discretion of the court," and derived from the French phrase *à merci.* For certain offences the penalty was *être mis à merci* (the Latin equivalent being *poni in misericordiâ) ;* and a person so punished was said to be *amercië* or *amerced.* Thus, in a passage quoted in Richardson's Dictionary from Rastall's " Abbreviacion of Statutes," A. D. 1520 : " Then al the articles of every hundred shall be delivered to the 12 jurors of the countie, and then time shall be appointed them to give their verdictes upon pain of the king's *mercie.* And, if they give not their verdictes, they shall bee *amerced* as to the justices shall seeme best."

Milton's Poetical Works, vol. iii. p. 127, ed. Masson.

Rastall.

Bigamy.

To base declension and loath'd *bigamy.*
King Richard III. Act iii. sc. 7.

" *Bigamy* signifies being twice married ; but is more justly denominated *polygamy*, or having a plurality of wives at once. Bigamy, according to the canonists, consisted in marrying two virgins successively, one after the death of the other, or once marrying a widow."

4 Bl. Comm. 163, note.

In " Romeo and Juliet," Act v. sc. 1, the Apothecary says :

> Such mortal drugs I have ; but Mantua's law
> Is death to any he that *utters* them.

Utter.

" *To utter* is a legal phrase often made use of in law proceedings and Acts of Parliament, and signifies to vend by retail."

Reed.

The word "attempt" has a very distinct meaning from " intent." An attempt is that which, if it had succeeded, would be the offence in question.

Attempt.

Intent.

C. C. 538, 551. Dearsly

> The *attempt* and not the *deed*
> Confounds us.
> *Macbeth,* Act ii. sc. 1.

The mere intention to commit a crime is not criminal. The law will not take notice

1 Hale P. C. 15.

of an intent without an act.   " Where there is no will to commit an offence, there can be no transgression."

In " Measure for Measure," Act. v. sc. 1, Isabella, beseeching the Duke, says : —

> My brother had but justice,
> In that he did the thing for which he died :
> For Angelo,
> His *act* did not o'ertake his bad *intent ;*
> And must be buried but as an intent
> That perish'd by the way : thoughts are no subjects,
> *Intents* but merely thoughts.

In the first scene of the third act of " King Richard II.," Bolingbroke says to Bushy and Green, you have —

Dispark.

> *Dispark'd* my parks, and fell'd my forest-woods.

Malone.

To *dispark* is a legal term, and signifies to divest a park, constituted by royal grant or prescription, of its name and character, by destroying the enclosures of such a park, and also the vert (or whatever bears green leaves, whether wood or underwood), and the beasts of chase therein, and laying it open.

In the third scene of the fourth act of
" The Taming of the Shrew," Tranio says :—

> My father is here look'd for every day,
> *To pass assurance* of a dower in marriage
> 'Twixt me and one Baptista's daughter here.

To pass assurance means to make a conveyance or deed. Deeds are by law-writers
called " The common assurances of the
realm " because thereby each man's property
is *assured* to him. So, in a subsequent
scene of this act, " they are busied about a
counterfeit *assurance.*"

In " King Henry VIII.," Act ii. sc. 4,
Queen Katharine says to Wolsey :—

> Therefore I say again,
> I utterly *abhor*, yea, from my soul
> *Refuse* you for my judge.

" These are not mere words of passion, but
technical terms in the canon law. *Detestor*
and *Recuso.* The former, in the language of
canonists, signifies no more than ' I *protest*
against;' the words are Holinshed's;—and

[margin: To pass assurance.]
[margin: Malone.]
[margin: Abhor.]
[margin: Refuse.]
[margin: Blackstone.]
[margin: Malone.]

therefore openly protested that she did utterly *abhor*, *refuse*, and forsake such a judge."

In "King Lear," Act ii. sc. 1, according to Lord Campbell, "there is a remarkable example of Shakespeare's use of technical legal phraseology." Gloucester says to Edmund, —

of my land,

Loyal and natural boy, I 'll work the means
To make thee capable.

Capable.

Lord Campbell.

In forensic discussions respecting legitimacy, the question is put, whether the individual whose status is to be determined is "capable," i. e. capable of inheriting; but it is only a lawyer who would express the idea of legitimizing a natural son by simply saying, —

I 'll work the means
To make him capable.

Determinate.

My bonds in thee are all *determinate.*
Sonnet LXXXVII.
So should that beauty which you *hold in lease*
Find no *determination.*
Sonnet XIII.

" Determinate," determined, ended. The term is used in legal conveyances; it is always used by lawyers instead of " ended."

King Richard says to Northumberland: —

Tell Bolingbroke, — for yond methinks he stands, —
That every stride he makes upon my land
Is dangerous treason : he is come to ope
The purple *testament* of bleeding war.

King Richard II. Act. iii. sc. 3.

Testament.

" I believe," says Steevens, " our author uses the word *testament* in its legal sense. Bolingbroke is come to open the testament of war, that he may peruse what is decreed there in his favour."

Steevens.

Metaphorical, beyond question, are these exquisite lines from Sonnet XXX. : —

When to the *sessions* of sweet silent thought
I *summon* up remembrance of things past.

Compare Dryden's noble use of " the last assizes " : —

Dryden.

The judging God shall close the book of fate,
And then *the last assizes* keep,
For those who wake and those who sleep.

Elegy on Mrs. Killegrew.

And these : —

But be contented ; when that fell *arrest*
Without all bail shall carry me away.

Sonnet LXXIV.

Addressing Malcolm, Macduff says : —

Great tyranny, lay thou thy basis sure,
For goodness dare not check thee ! wear thou thy wrongs,
Thy title is *affeer'd*.   *Macbeth*, Act iv. sc. 3.

Affeer.

Ritson.

" *To affeer*," says Ritson, himself a lawyer, " is to assess, or reduce to certainty. All amerciaments are by Magna Charta to be *affeered* by lawful men, sworn to be impartial. This is the ordinary practice of a Court Leet, with which Shakespeare seems to have been intimately acquainted, and where he might have occasionally acted as an *affeerer*."

Cowel, s. v. "Affeerers."

" Affeered " is a law term for confirmed. Thus in Cowel's Law Dictionary : " Affeerers may probably be derived from the French

affier, that is *affirmare, confirmare;* and signifies in the common law such as are appointed
in Court-Leets, upon oath, to set the fines
on such as have committed faults arbitrarily
punishable, and have no express penalty appointed by the statute."

ANTONIO. So please my lord the duke and all the court
To quit the fine for one half of his goods,
I am content ; so he will let me have
The other half *in use*, to render it,
Upon his death, unto the gentleman
That lately stole his daughter.

The Merchant of Venice, Act iv. sc. I.

In use. [marginal note]

In use, " That is, in trust for Shylock during
his life, for the purpose of securing it at his
death to Lorenzo. Some critics explain *in
use*, upon interest — a sense which the phrase
certainly sometimes bore ; but that interpreta-
tion is altogether inconsistent, in the present
passage, with the generosity of Antonio's character. In conveyances of land, where it is intended to give the estate to any person after
the death of another, it is necessary that

Anon. apud
Halliwell, fol. ed.
vol. v. pp.
443, 444. [marginal note]

a third person should be possessed of the
estate, and the *use* be declared to the one
after the death of the other; or the estate
to the future possessor would be rendered in-
secure. This is called a conveyance to *uses*,
and the party is said to be possessed, or
rather *seised* to the *use* of such an one, or to
the use that he render or convey the land to
such an one, which is expressed in law French
by the terms *seisie al use*, and in Latin, *seisi-
tus in usum alicujus*, viz. *A B or C D*. This
latter phrase Shakespeare has rendered with
all the strictness of a technical conveyancer,
and has made Antonio desire to have one
half of Shylock's goods in *use*, — to render
it upon his, Shylock's, death, to Lorenzo;
which is by no means an unfrequent mode of
securing a future estate, and in our author's
time nothing was more common than for A
to convey to B *in usum*, or to the *use* that he
should on a certain day enfeoff C or convey
to C. Suppose a gift to A et heredibus suis,
in usum, quod redderet B; and we have the
exact words of Antonio."

In " King Lear," Act iii. sc. 5, Cornwall, having created Edmund Earl of Gloucester, says to him : —

Seek out where thy father is, that he may be ready for our apprehension.

EDMUND. If I find him *comforting* the king, it will stuff his suspicion more fully.

Lord Campbell writes : " The indictment against an accessory after the fact, for treason, charges that the accessory ' comforted ' the principal traitor after knowledge of the treason." But there are no accessories in treason, because of the extreme gravity of the crime, and none in misdemeanor, because it is not worth while in misdemeanors to draw the distinction. Therefore in an indictment against several for treason or for a misdemeanor all are principals. In Hale's " Pleas of the Crown " it is said that " If A be indicted for treason and B for *comforting* and receiving him, it is true they are all principals," &c. The word has constantly been used in its technical sense. In the truce between England and Scotland in the reign of

Comforting.

Lord Campbell.

2 Hale P. C. 223.

Hall, " Richard III." fol. 19 a.

Richard III., it is provided that neither of the kings "shall maintain, favour, aid or *comfort* any rebel or traitor." And Bacon : " Not

" Observations upon a Libel," Life and Letters, vol. i. p. 194, ed. Spedding. See " King Lear," Clarendon Press ed. p. 173.

contented thus to have *comforted* and assisted her Majesty's rebels in England, he procured a rebellion in Ireland."

Shakespeare's knowledge of the practical administration of the law is shown in the following quotations from " Measure for Measure," and from " King Lear" : —

Juries.

The jury, *passing on* the prisoner's life,
May in the sworn twelve have a thief or two
Guiltier than him they try : What 's open made
To justice, that justice seizes : what knows the law
That thieves do *pass on* thieves ? 'T is very pregnant,
The jewel that we find, we stoop and take 't
Because we see 't ; but what we do not see
We tread upon, and never think of it.   Act ii. sc. 1.

To pass on.

" To pass on " that is to determine the guilt or innocence of the prisoner. In Spedding's

Bacon.

Letters and Life of Bacon, vol. ii. p. 283,

" King Lear," Clarendon Press ed. p. 177.

there is a list of " The Names of the Peers that *passed upon* the trial of the two Earls" of

Essex and Southampton. " To pass upon " is sometimes used in the sense of to pass sentence. Thus, in " King Lear," Act iii. sc. 7, Cornwall commands the attendants to bring in the traitor Gloucester, saying, —

> Though well we may not *pass upon* his life
> Without the form of justice.

Cf. " King Lear," Act iv. sc. 6 : —

Justices of the Peace.

> LEAR. A man may see how this world goes with no eyes. Look with thine ears : see how yond justice rails upon yond simple thief. Hark, in thine ear : change places ; and, handy-dandy, which is the justice, which is the thief?

The language of the court on the trial of questions of legitimacy, as reported in the Year Books, was sometimes more emphatic than decorous. Judge Richell improved upon the maxim of civil law in favor of legitimacy by making it of still more general application. He says, " For who that bulleth my cow, the calf is mine." Perhaps Shakespeare intended to immortalize Judge Richell and

Year Book, 7 Hen. iv. 9, 13. Barony of Gardner, lv. note.

his learned brethren, by making them the prompters of King John, in the following address to Robert Falconbridge : —

> KING JOHN. Sirrah, your brother is legitimate, —
> Your father's wife did after wedlock bear him ;
> And if she did play false, the fault was hers ;
> Which fault lies on the hazards of all husbands
> That marry wives. Tell me, how if my brother,
> Who, as you say, took pains to get this son,
> Had of your father claim'd this son for his?
> In sooth, *good friend, your father might have kept*
> *This calf, bred from his cow, from all the world ;*
> In sooth, he might : then, if he were my brother's,
> My brother might not claim him ; nor your father,
> Being none of his, refuse him : this concludes, —
> My mother's son did get your father's heir ;
> Your father's heir must have your father's land.
>
> > *King John*, Act i. sc. I.

1 Hale P. C. 425.

In Hale's Pleas of the Crown it is said that " Murder is a killing of a man ex malitiâ praecogitatâ." The words " malice afore-

Commonwealth *v.* Webster, 5 Cush. 306.

thought " do not imply deliberation or the lapse of considerable time between the malicious intent to take life and the actual execution of that intent, but rather denote purpose and design, in contradistinction to accident and mischance. In an indictment for murder it is necessary to allege that the act by which the death was occasioned was done of "malice aforethought," which is the great characteristic of the crime. In " The Winter's Tale," Leontes addressing Camillo says to him : —

> thou mightst bespice a cup,
> To give mine enemy a lasting wink ;
> Which draught to me were cordial.

Camillo answers : —

> Sir, my lord,
> I could do this, and that with no rash potion,
> But with a lingering dram, that should not work
> *Maliciously* like poison.   Act i. sc. 2.

" I should suppose," says Barrington, " that the word ' maliciously,' in this passage, is used in the sense it bears in the common forms of indictment for murder."

Observations on the Statutes, 527 note, 5th ed.

" Dowry," *dos mulieris*, otherwise called *maritagium*, or marriage goods, is that which the wife brings the husband in marriage. This word should not be confounded with

Dowry. 132 Mass. 275.

dower. An "assurance" is the legal evidence of the transfer of property. A "specialty" is a contract by deed. A "covenant," *convenant*, is an agreement, convention, or promise of two or more parties, by deed in writing, signed, sealed, and delivered, by which either of the parties pledges himself to the other that something is either done or shall be done, or stipulates for the truth of certain facts.

In the following conversation between Petruchio and Baptista, these technical terms are used with the precision of an experienced conveyancer : —

> PET. You knew my father well ; and in him, me,
> Left solely heir to all his lands and goods,
> Which I have better'd rather than decreas'd :
> Then tell me, — if I get your daughter's love,
> What *dowry* shall I have with her to wife?
> BAP. After my death, the one half of my lands ;
> And, in possession, twenty thousand crowns.
> PET. And, for that *dowry*, I 'll *assure her of*
> *Her widowhood*, — be it that she survives me, —
> In all my lands and leases whatsoever :
> Let *specialties* be therefore drawn between us,
> That *covenants* may be kept on either hand.
> *The Taming of the Shrew*, Act ii. sc. 1.

Petruchio, in consideration of the marriage settlement says, " I 'll assure her of her widow-hood," that is, will covenant that Katharina shall have her rights of dower, as his widow, in " all his lands and leases."

In all probability, Shakespeare's will was written by himself. It is expressed in terms at once apt and concise. The intention of the testator is abundantly manifest. On perusal, one is ready to exclaim with the Host in " The Merry Wives of Windsor," —

Shakespeare's Will.

> Thou art clerkly, thou art clerkly.

Without professional education and experience, the technical language of the law could not have been so appropriately used. In the interpolated clause making a bequest to his wife of personal property, he omits the technical word "devise" which he used in disposing of his realty, and says " I give," &c.

Burke, who had been educated for the bar, made his own will. His last days were clouded by the death of his only child, a son of great promise, and he desired to leave to his wife, absolutely, his entire estate, with no restrictions upon any part of it. His vocabulary was copious and famous. Of him it was first said, referring to his redundant adjectives, what, in our times, has been applied to Choate, "He drives a substantive and six." With this habit of language, and forgetting that he could not possibly accomplish his object so surely as by simply saying, "To my wife, Jane Mary Burke, *and her heirs*," he actually used instead of these last three technical words, seventy-one words, and then added the following forty-four words to clinch the seventy-one: "I hope these words are sufficient to express the absolute, unconditional, and unlimited right of complete ownership I mean to give her to the said lands and goods; and I trust, that no words or surplusage or ambiguity may vitiate this my clear intention." This was written in August 1794. But in July 1795, he made a codicil and devises the same lands over again to his "wife, Jane Mary Burke, and her *heirs* forever."

Burke's Will.

For a copy of this will, see Bissett's "Life of Burke," vol. ii. p. 440, 2d ed.

We thus have presented to our readers a portion of the evidence on the issue, whether or not Shakespeare was professionally versed in the " nice sharp quillets of the law,"

" And by their verdict [the issue] is determined."

If the verdict is in the affirmative, it may safely be concluded, that neither a motion in arrest of judgment nor a writ of error will lie.

NOTES.

NOTES.

—◆—

p. 22, l. 1. — "Ouster le main is a writ that is directed to the escheator, to deliver seisin or possession out of the king's hands unto the party that sues the writ, for that the lands seised are not holden of the king, or for that he ought not to have the wardship of them, or for that the king's title is determined, &c."

Termes de la Ley.

p. 22, l. 18. — "Attorney signifies in legal acceptation, one appointed by another man to do anything in his stead. Attorney is either general or special. Attorney general is he that by general authority is appointed to manage all our affairs or suits. Attorney special is he that is employed in one or more causes particularly specified. Attorney is seldom used now except of attorney at law."

Cowel.

In Trench's "Glossary" it is said that "attorney" is seldom used now except of the

Trench.

attorney *at law*. But formerly, any who in
any cause acted in the room, behalf, or turn of
another, would be called his "attorney." And
the writer cites the passage in the text in
support of this meaning.

p. 34, l. 18. — Walker (Critical Examination, &c.,
vol. iii. p. 14) would point "*cuckold! wittol!
cuckold!*"

Several.
Co. Litt. §§ 297,
298.
p. 39, l. 4. — "Also if lands be given to two to
have and to hold s[everally]." Mr. White's
conjecture, which he has introduced into the
text of Littleton, and distinguished by printing it in brackets, is not supported by authority. In "Littleton's Tenures in French and
English," printed in parallel columns, the word
in both columns is "scil.," which has its common and ordinary meaning. Sect. 298 in Coke
on Littleton (19th ed.) is as follows : "If lands
be given to two to have and to hold, *scil.* the
one moity to the one and to his heires, and
the other moity to the other and to his heires,
they are tenants in common." That this is
the true and only meaning (even if there could
be a doubt) is evident from the preceding sec-
tion (§ 297), in which the word "scil." in the
French column is rendered "viz." in the English. Co. Litt. § 297 runs thus : "Also, if

lands be given to an abbot and a secular man, to have and to hold to them, *viz.* to the abbot and his successors, and to the secular man to him and to his heires, they have an estate in common, causâ quâ suprâ."

p. 42, l. 2. — In Greene's "Quip for an Upstart Courtier," sig. D. 3d ed. 1620, there is a graphic description of a sergeant or sheriff's officer : " One of them had on a buffe-leather jerkin, all greasie before with the droppings of beere, that fell from his beard, and by his side, a skeine like a brewer's bung knife ; and muffled he was in a cloke, turn'd over his nose, as though hee had beene ashamed to showe his face." Dr. Johnson, in his Diction-ary, defines a bum-bailiff as "a bailiff of the meanest kind ; one that is employed in ar-rests." "It is painful to relate," says Lord Macaulay, "that, twice in the course of the year which followed the publication of this great work [his Dictionary], he was arrested and carried to spunging houses, and that he was twice indebted for his liberty to his excel-lent friend Richardson." *[marginal notes: Sheriff's officer. Johnson. Macaulay.]*

p. 43, last line. — See also the dialogue between Elbow and Lord Escalus, in " Measure for Measure," Act ii. sc. 1, as to the forms of action.

p. 45, l. 15.—These words were usual in indictments in Shakespeare's time (3 Inst. 59); and
they are retained in modern statutes and pre-
cedents of indictments.

p. 46, l. 17.—Beaumont and Fletcher founded
their play, "The Custom of the Country,"
upon this usage.

Statute
merchant.

p. 61, l. 10.—"The mercer, hee followeth the
young vpstart gentleman, that hath no gouerne-
ment of himselfe, and he feedeth his humour
to goe braue: hee shall not want silkes, sattins,
veluets, to pranke abroad in his pompe; but
with this prouiso, that hee must binde ouer his
land in *a statute merchant or staple:* and so
at last forfeit all unto the mercilesse mercer,
and leaue himselfe neuer a foot of ground in
England."—Greene, "Quip for an Upstart
Courtier," sig. F. 3. ed. 1620, quoted by Dyce,
ed. Middleton, vol. ii. p. 123 note.

1 Howell, 958; s.
c. 1 Phillipps, 21.

p. 66, l. 1.—During the trial of the Duke of Nor-
folk for high treason, in the year 1571, he
repeatedly requested that the witnesses for
the crown should be brought "face to face;"
and, on hearing the confession of the Bishop
of Ross read against him says: "it is of good
ground that I have prayed to have the Bishop
of Ross brought to me in private examination,

face to face, whereby I might have put him in remembrance of truth ; but I have not had him face to face, nor have been suffered to bring forth witnesses, proofs, and arguments as might have made for my purgation."

p. 66, l. 8. — John Owen *alias* Collins of Godstow in the county of Oxford was indicted and arraigned of high treason, for speaking there (among others) traitorous English words : " If the king be excommunicate by the pope, it is lawful for every man to kill him, and it is no murder," to which words he pleaded, Not guilty. And after the evidence was introduced, Cook, Chief Justice, said : " The matter of his indictment of treason was, his intent to compass the king's death. And notwithstanding that the words as to this purpose were but conditional, viz., 'If he were excommunicate,' yet it was treason. For proof of which this case was cited. The Duke of Buckingham, in the time of King Henry the Eighth said, 'That if the king should arrest him of high treason, that he would stab him with his dagger ;' and it was adjudged a present treason. And he said that in point of allegiance none must serve the king with *Ifs* and *Ands.* And afterwards Owen was found guilty, and judgment of treason was given."

Owen alias Collin's case, in the King's Bench, Godbolt, pl. 363, p. 263.

Leet.

p. 69, l. 2. — "Leet" also meant a day on which this court was held : —

> Keep *leets*, and law-days, and in session sit.
>
> *Othello*, Act iii. sc. 3.

p. 72, l. 14. — See the Preface to "The Riverside Shakespeare," vol. i. pp. xxi, xxii.

C. Elliot Browne
in "The Athe-
næum," 22 May,
1875.

p. 77, l. 14. — There is a striking imitation of this passage in Reynolde's "Dolarney's Primrose," 1606, quoted in the "New Variorum," vol. iii. p. 386 note : —

> " Why might not this haue beene some lawier's pate,
> The which sometimes brib'd, brawl'd, and tooke a fee
> And lawe exacted to the highest rate :
> Why might not this be such a one as he?
> Your quirks and quillets, now Sir, where be they?
> Now he is mute and not a word can say," &c.

Ritson.

p. 77, l. 22. — "A recovery with *double voucher* is the one usually suffered, and is so denominated from *two* persons (the latter of whom is always the common cryer, or some such inferior person) being successively *voucher*, or called upon, to warrant the tenant's title. Both *fines* and *recoveries* are fictions of law, used to convert an estate tail into a fee-simple."

Dante.

p. 79, l. 11. — " If He, which is the top of judgment." This expression " occurs in another great poet, one whose fame is as imperishable as Shakespeare's : "

Chè cima di giudicio *non s' avvalla,* &c.

Purgatorio, c. vi. 37.

quoted in Dyce's Shakespeare, vol. i. p. 485 note, 4th ed.

p. 89, l. 17. — The name of Mr. Justice Blackstone, the author of the "Commentaries," often occurs in the Third Variorum of 1821. "The notes which he gave me on Shakespeare," says Malone, "show him to have been a man of excellent taste and accuracy, and a good critic."

INDEX.

INDEX.

www.ingramcontent.com/pod-product-compliance
Lightning Source LLC
Chambersburg PA
CBHW032101010726
47493CB00008B/2490